84 STRANGE & AMAZING ANIMALS

KIDS WANT TO KNOW ABOUT

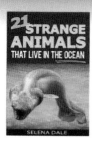

21 STRANGE ANIMALS THAT LIVE IN THE OCEAN

SELENA DALE

BOOK BUNDLE

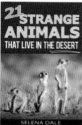

21 STRANGE ANIMALS THAT LIVE IN THE DESERT

SELENA DALE

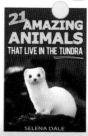

21 AMAZING ANIMALS THAT LIVE IN THE TUNDRA

SELENA DALE

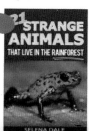

21 STRANGE ANIMALS THAT LIVE IN THE RAINFOREST

SELENA DALE

SELENA DALE

84 STRANGE and AMAZING ANIMALS KIDS WANT TO KNOW ABOUT

Weird & Wonderful Animals Collection

FOUR BOOKS IN ONE

Selena Dale

FREE GIFTS!

Just to say thank you for purchasing this book, I want to give you some free gifts.

Collect your free gifts here:

www.selenadale.com/get-your-free-gifts

Table of Contents

Introduction

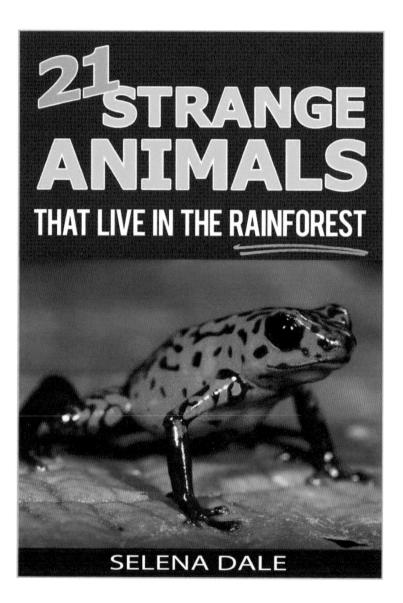

Introduction

Rainforests are amazing and beautiful. They contain more than half of the world's plant and animal species!

Rainforests are tall and very dense jungles that are teeming with awesome creatures. There are a lot of really strange animals that live in the rainy and very wet conditions of these huge forests. Many of them look as though they are from another planet and tend to have interesting habits.

Every year new and unusual animal species are being discovered which tells us there are even more strange creatures out there that we don't even know about...yet.

So what kind of weird and wonderful animals can we expect to find in different parts of the word?

What do these creatures look like and what do they eat?

What kind of habitat do they live in and most importantly...are they dangerous?

Sometimes an animal can look as though it is dangerous when in actual fact it is as gentle as a furry little kitten. Then again, there are animals that look so cute and cuddly yet they could be vicious killers!

So, here we have some strange animals that live in the rainforest. Some are a little weird, some are funny looking and some are dangerous but all of them are fascinating to learn about.

1. KINKAJOU

As inhabitants of the forests of Central and South America, Kinkajous are omnivores and are often found in trees.

Kinkajous are close relatives of raccoons and are sometimes called "Honey Bears" because they are fond of raiding the nests of bees.

They are nocturnal beings, which means that they eat and roam around at night and are often asleep during daytime.

FUN FACT: A Kinkajou's tail is very useful. It helps them hang on trees and helps in improving their balance as it easily grips on branches.

2. POISON DART FROG

You have to beware of the Poison Dart Frog as it is one of the most toxic animals on the planet. In fact, its venom is capable of killing at 10 least 10 adults!

They are also able to make use of their colors as it helps them ward of strangers and enemies.

But, no matter how seemingly "evil" they are, they are actually good and caring parents to their offspring— they carry their offspring with them on their backs!

FUN FACT: The Poison Dart Frog is named as such because American-Indian tribes were fond of using them to poison their arrows.

3. BULLET ANT

Small but definitely terrible, the Bullet Ant is known to give the most painful sting in the whole world.

The Bullet Ant is often found in Nicaraguan Rainforests and is often fat, club-shaped and reddish-black. Some people even think that they are wasps because they look almost the same way.

FUN FACT: A rite of passage ritual conducted by the Satre-Mawe tribe in Brazil includes asking young men to be bitten by bullet ants for 20 times in a day! Yikes!

4. JESUS LIZARD

The Jesus Lizard is also known as the Great Basilisk Lizard. It comes from the family of iguanas and is an excellent swimmer.

Its tail can also act as a whip in times of danger and helps protect it against enemies. An adult Jesus Lizard can grow up to 2 feet long.

FUN FACT: The Jesus Lizard got its moniker from Jesus. It is able to run on water, the way Jesus was able to walk on water—like a miracle of nature!

5. PEANUT HEAD BUG

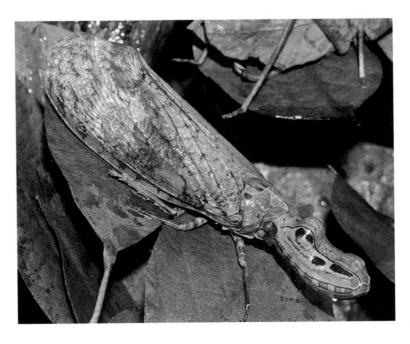

The Peanut Head Bug is named as such because its head resembles a peanut.

This works for them because predators think that they are not edible and so they choose to hunt for other prey. They also look like large bugs when their wings are spread out.

FUN FACT: While they may look terrifying, Peanut Head Bugs do not bite. All they can do is suck plant juices and that's why they rely on their weird appearance to keep them safe.

6. SATANIC LEAF TAILED GECKO

The Satanic Leaf Tailed Gecko often roams around the rainforests of Eastern Madagascar and really good at camouflaging themselves, making it hard for predators to find or notice them.

Its tail looks like a leaf and that's why it's so easy for it to blend with its surroundings. It is also often deemed as unique because of its physical appearance.

FUN FACT: While seemingly scary, the Satanic Gold Leaf Gecko is actually the smallest Gecko in the world!

7. PROBOSCIS MONKEY

The Proboscis Monkey is a very dominant type of monkey that is often found in the forests of Borneo.

They have webbed toes and the stomach of both males and females resembles a pot belly. They are full of fur that protect them from harsh weather conditions and also other animals.

FUN FACT: While you may think that its nose is ugly, it is actually what helps the Proboscis Monkey to find and attract a mate!

8. AYE-AYE

It is said that an Aye-Aye, (which is a type of lemur), is related to apes, chimpanzees and even humans.

They can be found in Madagascar and are mostly active at night. They eat insect larva, nectar, seeds, fruit and fungi.

They use their specially designed extra long middle finger to pick out food from inside tree trunks or hard shells.

FUN FACT: You won't find Aye-Ayes on the ground as they spend most of their lives clinging on to trees. They do not like going down and mingling with other animals.

9. GLASS FROG

At first you may think that the Glass Frog is just your average frog because it's in the color of lime green. But, take a good look at its stomach and you'll see that it is transparent, just like glass.

They often live near forest streams in Costa Rica and Central America and they are very active during daytime. They make use of that time to breed.

FUN FACT: You'll know that a frog is a glass frog if you see that its eyes are always facing forward and are very bright, especially during night-time.

10. POTOO

If you're traveling in Central and South America, you may already have come across a Potoo without knowing it. This is because a Potoo is one of the best animals in the world when it comes to camouflaging.

It could easily be mistaken for a small tree stump. These birds often lay their eggs on tree stumps to protect them from ground animals.

FUN FACT: While now common in South America, Potoos were first found in France and Germany 23 million years ago!

11. COLUGO

The Colugo is also known as the Sunda Flying Lemur and is often found in Borneo's jungles. They are great gliders and use the flaps between their legs to move from tree to tree.

Their teeth are quite destructive and they are nocturnal beings who are shy.

FUN FACT: As babies, Colugos spend around 6 months of their life clinging to their mother's bellies for protection.

12. AXOLOTL

A salamander that looks way different from other salamanders, the Axolotl is charming—due to its light pink (almost translucent) color, feathery gills and the fuzzes on its head.

Even when it has grown up, it still looks like a larva or a tadpole and are exclusively found in Xochimilco, Mexico.

They also tend to live in canals and lakes. They grow to up a foot long.

FUN FACT: Axolotls stay mainly underwater—unlike other salamanders who like to perch on rocks or on land, at times.

13. OKAPI

The Okapi is a Zebra Giraffe that is native to Congo. With their reddish-black body and white stripes, they look like zebras especially from a distance but are closer relatives of the Giraffe.

Like Giraffes, they are fond of eating buds and leaves of trees and don't like spending time with other animals.

FUN FACT: The Okapi has quite a long tongue. It uses its tongue to clean its ears (inside-out!) and even its eyelids!

14. RHINOCEROS HORNBILL

The Rhinoceros Hornbill is one of the largest of its kind and it can be found in Asian Rainforests.

It is popular for having red or orange irises and are often found inside tree trunks, especially if females are pregnant.

They are also quite protective of their hiding places, making sure that no other animals are able to go in.

FUN FACT: The Rhinoceros Hornbill is fond of eating small reptiles more than it likes fruits or insects.

15. DECOY-BUILDING SPIDER

A new species of spiders have recently been discovered in the Peruvian Amazon rainforests as part of the Genus Cyclosa.

The Decoy-Building Spider creates fake spiders and places them on their web in order to let predators think that these are real. The predators would come along and attack the decoy instead of the real spider.

FUN FACT: Interestingly enough, the decoy spiders do not just look like real spiders, they can also seem like they move! Weird!

16. CAPYBARA

Known as the largest rodent in the world, the Capybara is native to South America and is a close relative of guinea pigs.

They often roam around with a group of 10-100 Capybaras.

They are total herbivores who eat plants only and do not even like the smell of meat!

FUN FACT: Capybaras are awesome swimmers and divers. They can stay underwater for as long as 5 minutes!

17. THE PUSS CATERPILLAR

What makes the Puss Caterpillar different from other caterpillars is the fact that it is overly fuzzy and hairy.

The Puss Caterpillar is often found in the rainforests of Mexico and Central America. Be careful with this insect as its sting really hurts and can cause skin irritation and may even numb your limbs and bones!

FUN FACTS: It is usually gray or golden-brown and often looks like it hasn't brushed its hair. Now that's one animal that always has a bad hair day!

18. THE PINK DOLPHIN

Also known as the Pink Amazon River Dolphin, you cannot find dolphins such as this in the Ocean.

Aside from being Pink, sometimes they have flecks of brown or gray on their skin, too. They also should not be hunted as they are already close to extinction.

FUN FACTS: Pink Dolphins are the most intelligent of all dolphins! That's one more reason why they should be kept safe and taken care of.

19. 24 HOUR ANT

A close relative of the bullet ant, the 24 hour ant is infamous in Venezuela.

Their sting can truly hurt and may cause you to feel extreme pain and may make you feel numb for at least 24 hours, thus the name.

FUN FACT: While the Angel Falls is a popular tourist attraction in Venezuela, you have to be wary of 24-hour ants as they also frequent the place a lot.

20. HONDURAN WHITE BAT

The Honduran White Bat is probably the cutest and tiniest kind of bat that you will see. It has a white and fluffy coat and has almost no hair.

They are also called "leaf-nosed" bats at times because of the appearance of their nose and are often found in Nicaragua and the Honduras.

FUN FACT: The black membrane that covers their skull is quite useful: It is a natural form of sunscreen that protects them from the harsh rays of the sun!

21. MATA MATA

A large, freshwater turtle that is found in South Africa, the Mata-Mata is the only existing species in the Chelus Genus.

It is spiky and has large scales and often camouflages itself as a bark of a tree to ward off predators.

It uses its snout to breathe when it is in the water and is often found in stagnant pools or blackwater streams.

FUN FACT: While it has a large mouth, the Mata-Mata cannot chew and only swallows its food whole!

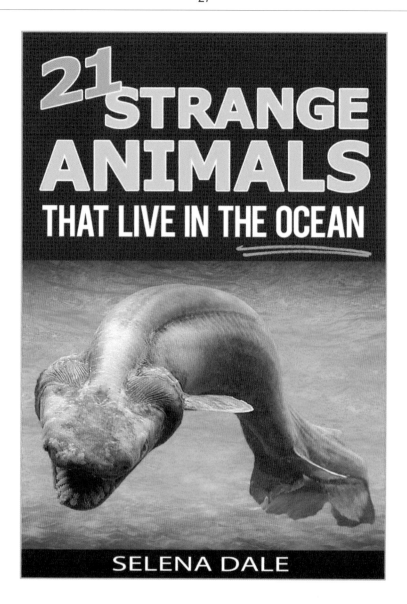

21 STRANGE ANIMALS THAT LIVE IN THE OCEAN

THAT LIVE IN THE OCEAN

SELENA DALE

Introduction

Around 70% of the Earth's surface is covered by oceans. Now that is a lot of oceans and a lot of water!

Some oceans you may have heard of are the Pacific Ocean, Atlantic Ocean, Indian Ocean, Arctic Ocean and the Southern Ocean.

So if there is so much water covering the Earth then there must be a huge amount of creatures living in them. There are hundreds of thousands of known marine life forms, but there are also thousands of creatures we still do not know about.

In this third book from the "Strange Animals Series" you will be able to see some of the amazing creatures that live in the ocean.

Some you may have seen before but there will be a fair few that look pretty strange and unusual too. In fact not all these creatures are found in parts of the sea that man can explore.

Some of these weird animals have been discovered many hundreds of feet deep in the dark and cold ocean.

You will see beauty and you will also see beasts. Many will make you giggle at how strange they look and a few may even scare you.

One thing is for sure and that is you will be fascinated by these truly amazing marine creatures.

22. SEA PENS

Sea Pens are peculiar invertebrate marine animals. There are around 300 species of Sea Pens. They can be found in both shallow and deep waters.

A species of Sea Pens called the Subselliflorae looks exactly like quill pens used for writing – hence their name.

Sea Pens are normally found rooted on the sea floor.

FUN FACT: Although they are hard to take care of, Sea Pens are sometimes sold for bigger aquariums.

23. BLOBFISH

The blobfish is a squishy, deep-sea fish that lives on the coasts of Australia, Tasmania, and New Zealand.

Usually, a blobfish doesn't grow any longer than 30 centimeters although this one in the picture obviously grew much bigger.

The blobfish's squishy body allows it to survive the high water pressure where it lives.

FUN FACT: The blobfish looks so ugly, it is considered as the world's ugliest animal.

24. PINK SEA-THROUGH FANTASIA

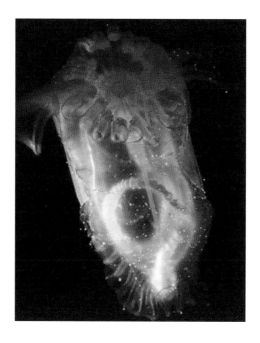

The strange Pink See-Through Fantasia is actually a sea cucumber with a pink, transparent body.

This weird creature lives 2,500 meters under the surface of the Celebes Sea. Pink See-Through Fantasia is a newly-discovered species.

FUN FACT: It moves around the water using its webbed feet located under their bodies.

25. THE SQUIDWORM

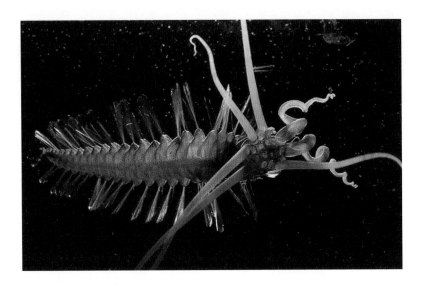

The Squidworm is another newly discovered species with a face that looks slightly creepy. The Squidworm is known to grow for up to 3.7 inches long.

Despite its name, it looks nothing like a worm or a squid. It has 10 tentacle-like appendages located on its head.

FUN FACT: It uses the appendages on its head to catch particles and detritus for food.

26. SEA ANGEL

The Sea Angel is a small sea slug that appears harmless at first look. These charming creatures look like they have transparent wings on the sides of their bodies.

These wings flap to help it move through the water. Despite their friendly name, Sea Angels are actually carnivores that eat other sea slugs and snails.

FUN FACT: The species of Sea Angels are very small that the largest known relative (the Clione Limacina) reaches only about 5 cm.

27. AXOLOTL

Axolotls, also called as Mexican salamanders or Mexican walking fish are four-legged creatures that can be found in many lakes.

They were also called "water monsters". Axolotls are amphibious creatures. However, adult Axolotls remain underwater and breathe using their gills.

They could grow for up to 15-45 cm in length. Since 2010, the Axolotls are in danger of extinction due to water pollution.

FUN FACT: The concept for a famous Pokémon called Mudkip was said to be based on the physical appearance of the Axolotl.

28. KIWA CRAB

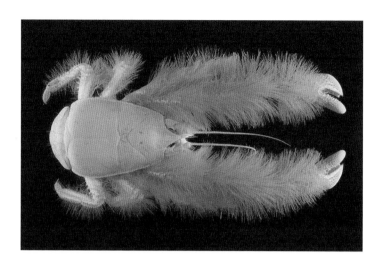

The Kiwa Crab or "Kiwa Hirsuta" is a strange-looking crustacean that was originally found in the South Pacific Ocean.

They can grow for about 5.9 inches in length. They are also called as "Yeti lobsters" or "Yeti crabs" due to the fur-like growth on its long pincers and legs.

FUN FACT: The 'hairs' or setae on the legs and pincers of the Kiwa crab contain bacteria that cleanse the water in hydrothermal vents where it lives.

29. PYCNOGONID SEA SPIDER

Pycnogonids or Sea spiders are the nightmare of people with arachnophobia. Despite its name and the usual eight legs, pycnogonids are not actually spiders.

They're not even considered as a member of the arachnids. There are also species of sea spiders with 10-12 legs.

FUN FACT: Due to extremely small size of some pycnogonids, they do not have respiratory systems.

30. FRILLED SHARK

The Frilled shark is a rare species of shark that can be found deep in the Atlantic and Pacific oceans.

These odd creatures are long with a strange, eel-like appearance. They are often observed with mouths widely open.

They can grow for up to 6.6 ft in length (about 2 meters).

FUN FACT: The Frilled Shark is named as such due to the long gill slits that appear like frills due to its extended gill filaments.

31. LONGHORN COWFISH

The strange, angular appearance of the longhorn cowfish is due to its hard carapace that protects most of its body.

They have a pair of long horns in front of its head; resembling a cow.

They are solitary creatures and are often territorial. Both male and female cowfishes have bright yellow color. They are known to excrete poison from their skin.

FUN FACT: The longhorn cowfish, just like others in the boxfish family, is a very slow swimmer. In fact, they can be caught by hand.

32. FLYING GURNARD

These strange large-eyed creatures can be found in the warm waters on both sides of the Atlantic Ocean.

The *flying gurnard* (also called *helmet gurnard*) are known for their large, wing-like pectoral fins that spread whenever they feel excited.

These slightly transparent fins also have phosphorescent blue coloration on the outer edges.

FUN FACT: Sometimes, flying gurnards "walk" on the sea floor to hunt for small invertebrates and crustaceans.

33. MOLA MOLA

The Mola mola or "ocean sunfish" is a large and very heavy species of fish.

They can grow for an average of 5.9 ft long and 8.2 ft high. The body of the Mola mola is flattened on the sides with two extended fins on top and below its body.

Mola molas eat large quantities of jellyfish to sustain its large body.

FUN FACT: The biggest and heaviest Mola mola ever recorded is over 10 feet high and weighed nearly 5,000 pounds!

34. BLUE DRAGON

The "Glaucus atlanticus" or Blue Dragon is a species of very small sea slugs.

An adult blue dragon can grow for up to 3 cm long. It has a long, silver stripe running down the length of its body.

Its six appendages have several other 'fingers' that look like wings when extended.

FUN FACT: Touching these tiny creatures may cause a painful sting due to the nematocysts stored in their bodies.

35. CARPET SHARK

Carpet sharks (also called as Wobbegongs) are species of sharks that have patterned colorations on top of their bodies.

Some carpet sharks use their patterns as camouflage.

FUN FACT: Carpet sharks spend most of their time lying on the sea floor; displaying their patterned bodies just like carpets.

36. SEA PIG

A sea pig or Scotoplanes is a strange looking creature with a pink, rounded appearance.

They grow for about 6 inches in length; resembling a large potato. They can be found in the Atlantic, Pacific, and Indian oceans.

They eat organic particles found on the sea floor. The legs at the base of their bodies and their pink skins are what contribute to their pig-like appearance.

FUN FACT: The Sea pig's legs are used by the creature to put food into its mouth.

37. RED-LIPPED BATFISH

These strange and slightly disturbing creatures can be found near Cocos Island off the shore of Costa Rica.

They are also called Galapagos batfish. These unusual creatures use their fins to 'crawl' across the ocean floor. They eat mostly smaller fishes and crustaceans.

FUN FACT: Just like the Anglerfish, the Red-lipped batfish also has an elongated structure on its head called the illicium.

38. MANTIS SHRIMP

The Mantis shrimp or stomatopods are brightly colored crustaceans that can be found in the tropics and sub-tropics.

They were also called as "sea locusts" and "thumb splitters". Mantis shrimps can grow for up to 12 inches in length.

The Mantis shrimp is known for its very powerful claws that deliver damage using a punching motion.

FUN FACT: Some bigger species of mantis shrimp are known to break through aquarium glass by 'punching' it with its claws.

39. NARWHAL

The Narwhal or "Narwhale" belongs to a species of medium-sized whales.

Their bodies can grow for up to 5.5 meters and weighs for up to 1,600 kilograms.

They can be found in the Canadian Arctic and Greenlandic seas. They are known for the long 'tusks' in front of their heads.

FUN FACT: Narwhals are known to communicate with each other using "clicks", "whistles", and "knocks".

40. MIMIC OCTOPUS

Octopuses are known for their ability to change skin color. However, the Mimic Octopus or "Thaumotctopus Mimicus" is capable of using its flexible body to copy the bodies of other sea creatures.

They often mimic corals and rocks to avoid predators.

FUN FACT: The Mimic octopus is intelligent enough to identify which animal or object to imitate when facing various threats.

41. MEGAMOUTH SHARK

These extremely rare species of sharks lives in the depths of the Pacific, Atlantic, and Indian oceans.

When feeding, the Megamouth shark swims through the water with its large mouth wide open. It feeds mainly on plankton and jellyfish.

They can grow for up to 5.5 meters long and weigh for up to 1,215 kilograms. In average, their mouths can measure for up to 1.3 meters.

FUN FACT: The Megamouth shark is extremely rare that only 58 sharks were ever caught or sighted.

42. CHIMAERA

The Chimaeras are believed to be the oldest group of fishes today. They live 8,500 feet from the surface of temperate oceans.

The Rhinochimaeridae or long-nosed chimaera is known for its long snout and its set of sharp teeth.

They have branched off from the shark species around 400 million years ago.

FUN FACT: A slightly disturbing photo of a long-nosed chimaera circulated around the internet was mistaken as a Goblin shark.

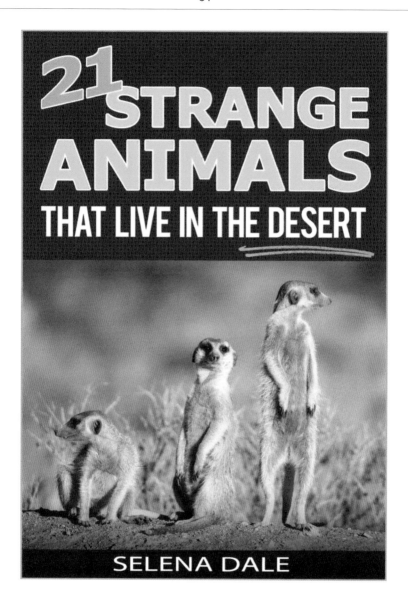

Introduction

Deserts are large hostile enviornments that are found in many parts of the world. They are barren areas of land that get very little rainfall per year.

There are 4 categories of desert:

- **Subtropical Deserts** which are the hottest and driest.
- **Cool Coastal Deserts** which are cooler due to being near the ocean.
- **Cold Winter Deserts** have temperatures that change from very hot to very cold in different seasons.
- **Polar Deserts** which have freezing temperatures.

Most of the amazing animals in this book are from the hotter climate deserts such as the Subtropical and Coastal deserts.

Around one third of the Earth's surface is covered in deserts but only 20% of them are covered in sand. There are over 30 major deserts, not including the smaller ones, and all of them have some form of animal and plant life.

So how does an animal survive in such extreme conditions? What type of animals could even endure the hot sun during the day and the freezing cold during the night?

What about those really strange looking sea creatures that live in the oceans of the coastal deserts?

43. HORNED VIPER

Desert Horned Vipers are hard to find because they bury themselves in the sand to protect themselves from the desert heat.

They have horns that stick out above their eyes for protection especially when they burrow underground.

They can't dig holes though; they borrow the holes created by other desert animals like lizards.

FUN FACT: When threatened, Desert Horned Vipers will rub their scales together to produce a saw-like sound.

44. DUNG BEETLE

Dung beetles survive by eating the feces of other animals. They find it using their keen sense of smell.

They usually stay where the feces are, but if they're taking care of children they roll it around and take it home.

FUN FACT: Dung beetles are suspected to navigate by looking at the sky. They use the galaxy as their guide especially when bringing their rolled feces home.

45. FENNEC FOX

The Fennec fox is the world's smallest fox, standing only at about eight inches tall.

They have large, six-inch ears for finding prey underground. Their furry paws protect them from the hot sand.

They usually burrow underground in the morning when it's hot and come out to hunt at night when it's cold.

FUN FACT: Fennec foxes can live without water indefinitely and can survive on the moisture they get from their food.

46. DEATHSTALKER SCORPION

Deathstalker scorpions get their name from their highly toxic venom.

Their pinchers aren't very powerful but a sting from them can be very fatal.

Their colors depend on where they live in, primarily because they want to blend in so they don't get seen.

FUN FACTS: The smaller the pincers of the Deathstalker scorpion, the more poisonous the venom is.

47. MONITOR LIZARD

Monitor lizards are often very large creatures that can grow up to seven feet long.

Most of them are great swimmers and have strong claws and tails for lashing out prey.

They're very intelligent and some people even say that they recognize their owners.

FUN FACT: Monitor lizards have forked tongues they use for detecting the scents of their prey.

48. THE JERBOA

Jerboas are small, mouse-like animals with very large ears.

The color of their fur coat depends on their environment to help hide them from predators.

They're pretty shy and will often live on their own burrow.

FUN FACT: Even with a maximum of about six inches, Jerboas can jump up to about ten feet when threatened by a predator.

49. HONEYPOT ANTS

It's pretty hard to find food in the desert so when honeypot ants find food they turn themselves into storage pots and eat as much as they can.

They can feed other hungry ants from the same colony by throwing up into the hungry ant's mouth.

FUN FACT: When Honeypot ants have eaten enough food, they hang on walls to wait for other hungry ants to feed.

50. AUSTRALIAN THORNY DEVIL

Australian thorny devils truly deserve their name because of their scaly, rough, spiky skin.

Despite their intimidating appearance, they're pretty small and eat about 3,000 ants a day.

They have a false, spiky head that acts as a decoy to keep away predators

FUN FACT: Australian thorny devils get water by moving around moist places and allowing their body to move the water to their mouths.

51. DESERT KIT FOX

Desert kit foxes are furry little animals that have yellowish sandy coats to help blend in the desert environment.

They can have quick bursts of speed, but they can't run for too long. They usually hunt their prey by either stalking them or digging them out from their burrows.

FUN FACT: Desert kit foxes hide in dens created by other animals or even humans as protection from the winter or the summer.

52. RED TAILED HAWK

Red tailed hawks are carnivorous birds whose diet consists mostly of rodents.

They tend to have the same territories throughout their lives and rarely migrate. They create nests that other small birds sometimes rest in.

FUN FACT: Red tailed hawks make shrill sounds that are often used as raptor sounds in movies.

53. SHREW

Shrews are mole-like mammals very fragile in nature.

Their heart beats at about 800 times a minute and could easily be startled to death literally by sudden noise.

They won't make it through the day without eating because of their fast metabolism.

FUN FACT: Shrews could eat up to 2-3 times its own weight in food and will have to keep eating to stay alive.

54. SLOTH BEAR

Sloth bears are long-haired, fuzzy bears that have long snouts and strong claws for digging and sucking up insects.

They're pretty active during the night noisily ravaging trees and other debris for fruits and insects.

FUN FACT: The noise sloth bears make when they eat can be heard from over 300 feet away due to the flaps of their nose preventing dirt from mixing with its food.

55. HYRAX

Rock hyraxes are relatives of manatees and dugongs despite looking like giant rodents.

They're usually found in rock formations and other hard to reach areas.

They are very territorial and have glands on their backs that secrete odors to mark their territories.

FUN FACT: Rock hyraxes can compose complex songs with different sounds like birds. They do this usually for territorial reasons

56. MEERKAT

Meerkats are highly social mongooses often found living in packs.

They have excellent long-range eyesight for guarding and foraging although their short-rage eyesight is quite poor.

They are immune to the poison from snakes and scorpions.

FUN FACT: Meerkats could whip up a cloud of dust to protect themselves from predators and can easily dash for cover, running up to 37 miles per hour.

57. GREATER ROADRUNNER

Greater roadrunners are interesting birds that come from a family of cuckoos.

They can run up to 20 miles per hour and can fly for a very short time.

They eat various animals such as mice, lizards, and even poisonous snakes and scorpions.

FUN FACT: Greater roadrunners can hunt down and eat rattlesnakes by finding another roadrunner to distract the snake while it aims for its head.

58. CHUCKWALLA

Chuckwallas are large lizards that enjoy hiding in rocky places.

The males excrete scent through their glands to mark their territory and will not tolerate other males from entering their territory.

They mostly eat plants but will start eating insects if they can't find enough vegetation.

FUN FACT: When running away isn't enough to keep away predators, they inflate their stomachs while in-between rocks to keep them from being pulled away.

59. KANGAROO RAT

Kangaroo rats are actually small rodents that hop a lot like a kangaroos.

Unlike most kangaroos, they don't keep their babies in their pouches; the pouches outside their cheeks are used to bring food back to their homes.

They live in very organized burrows that have specific chambers for eating, sleeping, etc.

FUN FACT: Kangaroo rats can convert the seeds they eat into water whenever needed.

60. CARACAL

Caracals are small cats sometimes called "Desert lynxes" or "African lynxes".

They have large ears to help them detect prey miles away.

They hunt during the night and sleep during the day so they won't suffer in the desert heat.

FUN FACT: Caracals can live for a long time without drinking water by getting moisture from their prey.

61. PEREGRINE FALCON

Peregrine falcons are one of the largest species of birds known to exist.

They often feed on small birds and ducks and will often catch them mid-air.

A lot of them now live in cities where the buildings are tall enough to build a nest in.

FUN FACT: Peregrine falcons can reach 200 miles per hour when they swoop down to catch their prey. This makes them one of the fastest animals on record.

62. LOCUST

Locusts are pretty famous due to their invasions on farms.

They could easily jump up to as high as 2.3 feet and some could even fly at a speed of about 10 miles per hour.

The desert locust can cover as much as about 460 square miles in swarm.

FUN FACT: When locusts bump into each other, a swarm begins and eventually the next generations start changing their shape and color.

63. WALKING STICK

Walking sticks blend into the environment because of their grass or wood-like appearance.

Their diet consists of plant leaves or stems, which they eat at night.

They can let go of their limbs when a predator tries to grab it and regenerate a new one.

FUN FACT: Eggs of walking sticks are also camouflaged, often colored brown.

Introduction

The Tundra is a huge expanse of flat and treeless ground that can be found in tha Arctic regions of Europe, Asia and North America.

The environment has frosty landscapes in very low temperatures. It is a cold barren wasteland that includes snow, rocks and very little variety in vegetation.

The tundra is an unusually cold and dry climate with strong and drying winds. This is not a place for ordinary animals to live.

This is a place where only the strongest will survive and that means animals with the best protection against the powerful cold winds and freezing temperatures.

Some of these animals are big and some are small. Some are predators and others are scavengers. Some live in the ocean, some live above ground and some live below ground.

All of them have their own unique ways of tackling the unforgiving weather and they are all experts in finding food for survival.

For many of the above ground animals it is about day to day survival to find food, water and shelter.

Take a look at some of these amazing animals that live in one of the most inhospitable climates on Earth.

64. WOLVERINE

Also called by the Blackfeet Indians as "skunk bear", the wolverine is the largest of the terrestrial or land-living weasels.

It is a big weasel that looks like a small bear. The wolverines are solitary animals, meaning they like being alone.

They are mostly found in Canada, Alaska in USA, Russia and Siberia.

They are known for being stronger and fiercer than they look.

FUN FACT: Did you know that even though wolverines are dark-colored, their babies are pure white!

65. CANADA LYNX

The Canada Lynx is a North American mammal. It is a wild cat that is usually two times the size of pet cats!

It is a secretive and mostly nocturnal animal. Nocturnal means that even if it can be awake anytime, it likes moving around at night.

They are known for running very fast but they get tired easily.

FUN FACT: Did you know that a big group of lynx can hunt down big animals like deer?

66. ARCTIC HARE

Also called the "polar rabbit", the arctic hare is a mammal that lives in the polar region by the help of their thick, white fur.

It is a big, white rabbit that digs holes in the snowy ground to make tunnels to their warm home.

They are mostly found in Greenland and Canada, but some are found in Labrador.

FUN FACT: Did you know that a mommy arctic hare can have up to eight babies called "leverets".

67. RED FOX

The red fox is the biggest among the true foxes. They like living where there are people.

Being a carnivore, the red fox eats meat. And even if they are called the red fox, not all red foxes are red. There are white and brown too.

They are mostly found in the cold countries, but there are also a lot of red fox in Australia! They live in burrows like rabbits and the children stay with their parents as long as they are not married.

FUN FACTS: Did you know that the red fox, because of their fur, is also sometimes called the fire fox?

68. BELUGA WHALE

Also called the white whales, are the closes relative of the narwhal or the sea unicorns. They are also called the "melon head"

They live around the Arctic where the water is very cold.

The front of their head has a bump that is called the "melon". It is very squishy. They can bump on a wall without hurting their head.

Their flippers are wide and short, making them look square-shaped.

FUN FACT: Did you know that as the beluga grows older, their tails become more curved?

69. POLAR BEAR

Their scientific name means "maritime bear" or sea bear.

They live in the Arctic Circle, like in Canada, Russia and the North Pole.

Also called the "Nanook", they eat fish and other small animals in their territory.

Because of the Global Warming, the polar bears are slowly losing their home.

FUN FACT: Did you know that polar bears have black skin beneath their snow white fur? And they get drunk by sniffing gas fuel.

70. CARIBOU

Also called the reindeer, it is smaller than its cousins, the moose.

They live mostly in Alaska and Canada.

They use their sharp hooves to get moss and lichen – their favorite food, also called the reindeer moss.

Caribou antlers (or growing horns) have a smooth and soft fur-like covering called velvet.

FUN FACT: Did you know that their hooves change shape depending on the seasons? Soft in summer and harder in winter!

71. SNOWY OWL

One of the larger birds in the owl family, the snowy owl is the official bird of the province of Quebec in Canada.

One of the biggest owls around, the snowy owl has a black beak and bright yellow eyes. They have white feathers that are sometimes spotted or striped with black or gray.

They are mostly found in Canada, Alaska in USA, and other cold European countries. They eat other small birds and mammals, but sometimes, they will settle for fish or frogs.

FUN FACT: Did you know that Hedwig from the Harry Potter series is a snowy owl named Ook?

72. DUSKY DOLPHIN

Named because of their almost pure black skins, they are related to the white-side dolphin.

They are small to medium if compared to other dolphins, but they loved to jump and turn somersaults in the air.

They swim in the waters of South America, Africa, and Australia.

They like eating fish and especially giant squids.

FUN FACT: Did you know that dolphins know where they are by making clicking and buzzing sounds like bats do?

73. GYRFALCON

The gyrfalcons are the biggest among all the falcons in the world.

With their feathers colored differently from white to brown, their name means vulture falcon, because of the similarity in colors.

They are mostly found in North America, Greenland and North Europe. They are the national symbol of Iceland.

FUN FACT: Did you know that Vikings treat gyrfalcons as great guardian birds!

74. ARCTIC FOX

Also known by other names such as the white fox and the polar or snow fox, they are small foxes native to the Arctic region.

They feed on any other small animals they could find. They are monogamous meaning couples stay together forever.

They are usually found in the edges of Greenland, Russia, Canada, Alaska in the USA and Scandinavia.

They are the only land mammal that can be found originally in Iceland.

FUN FACT: Did you know that snow foxes have white fur in winter that turns to brown during the summer?

75. RIBBON SEAL

A medium size member of the true seal family, they can only stay in the areas where there is always ice.

They are known because of their fur color and pattern: they have two wide strips and two circles that are white on their dark brown or black fur.

They only eat fish, squids and octopuses. They can dive up to 200 meters below the water surface.

FUN FACT: Did you know, not like the other seals, ribbon seals do not form herds, instead staying only with their partner and babies.

76. MUSK OX

Named because of the odor their bodies produced during some seasons, the musk ox are more related to sheep than to other oxen.

They have long curving horns present on both males and females. They have long, warm and soft wool.

They are now mostly found in Greenland and eastern Canada.

FUN FACT: Did you know that although all other musk oxen are black or brown, there are white musk oxen found in the Queen Maud Gulf Bird Sanctuary!

77. ERMINE

Also known as the stoat or the short-tailed weasel, they are different from weasels because of their short tails.

A male ermine is called a jack while a female is the jill. They do not make their own burrows and nests; instead, they re-use abandoned nests and burrows.

They are very common in the northern countries and also in New Zealand.

FUN FACT: Did you know that ermine actually refers to the stoat's pure white winter coat of fur?

78. BOWHEAD WHALE

It is a fat, dark-colored whale without a dorsal fin. They have also been called the arctic whale or the Russian whale.

They are slow swimmers that can stay under the water without inhaling for as long as 40 minutes.

They can now be found mostly in the waters of Canada, Alaska and West Greenland.

FUN FACT: Did you know that bowhead whales have the largest mouths of any animal alive on earth?

79. CHINSTRAP PENGUIN

They are small penguins found in Antarctica, Deception Island, South Shetland and other barren islands.

Even though they live in uninhabited islands, during winter, they all meet in icebergs. They are the most aggressive to outsiders among all the penguins.

Like the other small penguins, they build circle nests with smalls tones and pebbles and lay two eggs. Baby chinstrap penguins are grey.

FUN FACT: Did you know their name came from their colors that look as if they are wearing black helmets with chinstraps?

80. GRAY WOLF

They are what are commonly called the timber wolves. They are different than the other wolves because, like the red wolf, they are bigger.

They hunt large prey like deer, moose, bison, oxen and other ungulates or animals with hooves.

They are one of the most popular wolves so many of them are found all over the world both in reserve areas and in the wild.

FUN FACT: Even if wolves usually hunt in groups called packs, there are times when even one grey wolf can kill a large prey like a moose.

81. ELEPHANT SEAL

They are large, earless seals that like to swim in the ocean.

Elephant seals have babies once a year and stay in the same group called colony all their life.

They eat so much fish every time they dive because their very large bodies make it difficult to climb in and out of the ocean.

FUN FACT: Did you know that their name comes from the males having longer noses than normal seals, like elephant trunks?

82. LEMMINGS

Lemmings are small rodents that can only be found in or near the Arctic where it is almost always cold.

They are subnivean animals, meaning they live in the tunnels formed underneath the snow by melting and re-freezing.

Unlike other animals, they do not hibernate during very cold winters. They remain active all the time by nibbling on food they find or stored in their tunnel homes.

FUN FACT: Did you know that lemmings are different from other rodents because instead of being shy and scared, they become aggressive when in danger!

83. ARCTIC GROUND SQUIRREL

They are ground squirrels that live in the arctic north, especially in Canada, Alaska and Siberia.

They live in shallow burrows they make on the ground in river banks, mountain slopes and lake shores.

They rub noses when they meet friend and make "tsk-tsk" sounds when they meet enemies.

FUN FACT: Did you know that they are also called Parka? And the jacket style called parka was named after them.

84. GRIZZLY BEAR

They are brown bears that live in North America. They are also called silver-tips because that's how their fur looks like up-close.

Even if bears are definitely meat-eaters, grizzlies are omnivores. That means they eat mixed plants and meat. Depends on what is available.

Canadian and Alaskan grizzly bears are larger than the American grizzlies.

FUN FACT: Did you know that grizzly cubs stay with their mom for two years, then after that, they try to avoid her all the time?

THE END

Check Out My Other Books

Just go to Amazon and search for "Selena Dale Books"

OR

Got to www.selenadale.com

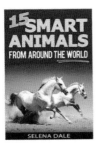  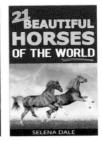

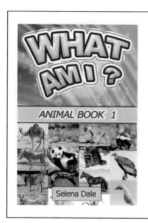
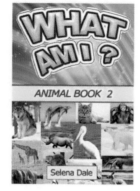
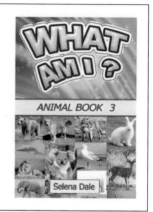

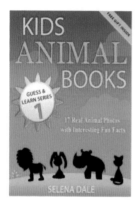
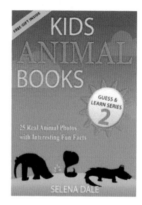
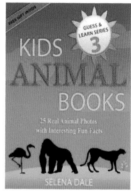

About Selena

Selena Dale was born in United Kingdom, London and has lived there most of her life. She has a passion for writing and loves to learn new things, especially if she can share what she has learned with her two children.

Due to her varied interests and love of writing she decided to create children's books. She can now pick and choose any topic to write about while sharing what she has written with her kids.

"Young children's brains are like sponges, ready to absorb all that wonderful knowledge. A child who loves to read is a child whose imagination will be flexed like a muscle. Now that is a pretty good foundation."

Selena Dale

IMAGE SOURCE AUTHOR CREDITS

AT http://commons.wikimedia.org UNLESS OTHERWISE STATED

Wolverine - michiganexposures.blogspot.com
Canada Lynx - Keith Williams
Arctic Hare - Steve Sayles
Red Fox - Peter Trimming
Beluga Whale - savenaturesavehuman.blogspot.com
Snowy Owl - Floyd Davidson
Musk Ox - Quartl
Elephant Seal - Mike Baird
Chinstrap Penguins - Gilad Rom
Gyrfalcon - Ólafur Larsen
Lemmings - thejunglestore.blogspot.com
Ermine - www.animalstown.com
Arctic Ground Squirrel - canadafurandfeathers.blogspot.com
Bowhead Whale - jollydiver.com
Gray Wolf - wolf.org
Grizzly Bear - www.donaldmjones.com
Kinkajou - hugeinhongkong.blogspot.com
Poison Dart Frog - newswatch.nationalgeographic.com
Bullet Ant - www.myrmecos.net
Jesus Lizard - Tubifex
Peanut Head Bug - Hectonichus
Potoo - jordylakiere.deviantart.com
Satanic Leaf-Tailed Gecko - storify.com
Proboscis Monkey - David Dennis
Rhinoceros Hornbill - Steve Wilson
Aye-Aye - franslanting.photoshelter.com
Okapi - Charles Miller
Capybara - Karelj
Puss Caterpillar - hortipm.tamu.edu

The Pink Dolphin - conniemudore.blogspot.com
Colugo - Lip Kee Yap
Honduran White Bat - Geoff Gallice
Blobfish - www.welikethat.de
Squidworm - Teuthidodrilus
Frilled Shark - rwbyfanon.wikia.com
Flying Gurnard - Beckmannjan
Mola Mola - Per-Ola Norman
Blue Dragon - digitaljournal.com
Sea Pig - www.catinwater.com
Red-Lipped Batfish -www.modern-age-studio.com
Mantis Shrimp - dive.nl
Narwhal - blog.dedoles.sk
Horned Viper - Holger Krisp
Dung Beetle - Kay-africa
Deathstalker Scorpion - Yair Goldstof
Monitor Lizard - FlyingToaster
Fennec Fox - Tim Parkinson
Jerboa - boneeater
Australian Thorny Devil - KeresH
Desert Kit Fox - B. Peterson
Meerkat - Sara&Joachim&Mebe
Kangaroo Rat - Dolovis
Greater Roadrunner - Madmaxmarchhare
Chuckwalla - Adrian Pingstone
Sloth Bear - Asiir
Red-Tailed Hawk - www.howardsview.com
Peregrine Falcon - uglybugga.deviantart.com
Walking Stick - Fritz Geller-Grimm and Felix Grimm

Copyright Information

Published in the United States by SELENA DALE

©SELENA DALE
Copyright 2014

Made in the USA
Lexington, KY
22 October 2016